# The Art of
# STUBBORNNESS

- - - - - - - - - - - - - - - -

Nancy McLoughlin

WestBow
PRESS
A DIVISION OF THOMAS NELSON

WestBow Press books may be ordered through booksellers or by contacting:

WestBow Press
A Division of Thomas Nelson
1663 Liberty Drive
Bloomington, IN 47403
www.westbowpress.com
1-(866) 928-1240

ISBN: 978-1-4497-1898-5 (sc)
ISBN: 978-1-4497-1899-2 (e)
Library of Congress Control Number: 2011931026

Printed in the United States of America

WestBow Press rev. date: 6/13/2011

# TABLE OF CONTENTS

## Chapter One

# INTRODUCTION OF ARTHUR STONE

Meet my friend, Arthur Stone, a man who has an interesting past. Like many people, he struggled with the sin of stubbornness, although he would never admit it. He was a smart guy, and very addicted to following his own thought processes. He was convinced he knew what was best for him AND for everyone else if they would just listen to him! He believed he could figure out problems on his own and didn't need the help of others, and sometimes that was true! He was positive he'd made the best choices for himself throughout his life; after all, who knew and cared about him better than himself? So, of course, he would be the expert on what he should do at all times.

Art grew up in a home where his parents were very busy and allowed him great freedom to make his own choices. He developed a sense of dependence on himself because there really was no one else he could lean on. He figured out early in life that if he DID trust or depend on someone else, that person would eventually let him down. He was rarely punished because his parents were preoccupied with their own lives, and besides, they thought he was just going through a stage, and that he'd outgrow it. Between the lack of self-discipline resulting from this type of parenting and the lack of boundaries and training he received, Art was left clueless on how to approach life. Eventually he set up his own thoughts as his compass and used them to guide every part of his life. Armed with just his perception of the way things should be, he began navigating through such land minds as friendships, marriage, parenting, and careers.

It was his friends, acquaintances, spouse, and employees who began calling him "The Rock." They said it was easier to move a huge rock than to change Art's mind once he decided on a particular course of action. Instead of reading the dictionary definition of stubbornness and seeing how well it fit (**unreasonably obstinate; obstinately unmoving; fixed or set in purpose or opinion; resolute; hard, tough, or stiff as stone or wood; difficult to shape or work; perversely unyielding**), Arthur would use words to describe himself like strong, persistent, determined, and RIGHT! He couldn't understand why those around him didn't think like he did, but since he was so sure he was right and they were wrong, he began distancing himself from anyone who didn't agree with him. He justified his actions of steam-rolling over the "opposition", lying to get his way, manipulating people and situations, and ignoring the damage being done to his relationships. "After all," he soothed his conscience, "It's their fault for not listening to me."

One day his wife left because she could no longer handle always being "wrong." His kids began to shut him out of their lives until they became strangers to him. After awhile his employees, one-by-one, began refusing to work for him and sought employment elsewhere. His boss finally terminated him because Art continually stood up to him instead of having a "team player" attitude. Art became bitter and angry, stymied as to why people were so foolish that they couldn't see the wisdom of his decisions and words. As he sat alone and ignored, he wondered aloud, "What went wrong?"

-------------------------------------------

**1.** Do you see bits and pieces of the above scenarios creeping into or perhaps firmly established in your life? Does it shock you to think what you thought was everyone else's problem or fault, could be, at least partly, yours? Explain the kinds of situations that cause this stubbornness to show up in your life? _____

_____

_____

_____

\* Is the word "stubborn" hard to swallow? If so, meditate on it a bit and then come back to the questions.

**2.** IF you are a stubborn person, can you see how your behavior is affecting those around you? _____

_____

_____

_____

**3.** Now that you've begun to process the possibility of you having stubborn traits (or being stubborn), on a scale of 0 – 10, how would you rank your stubbornness quotient? Why? _____

_____

_____

_____

**4.** Do you know anyone like Art? What characteristics make them stubborn? What actions make them stubborn? Do you see any similar characteristics in yourself? Has anyone ever mentioned to you that stubborn traits you see in others can also be seen in you? How did you receive that comment? _____

_____

_____

_____

**5.** If stubbornness began in your early years, could a different kind of parenting experience have produced the same (stubborn) results seen in Art? If so, what might those experiences look like? (Examples: permissiveness, abuse, rigidness, etc.) _____

_____

_____

_____

**6.** Why do parenting styles affect children to such a degree, either negatively or positively? _____

_____

_____

_____

**7.** Did your childhood make you stubborn or is it an innate part of your particular nature? Explain. _____

_____

_____

_____

**8.** Can you imagine the idea that negative consequences, results, or effects could be mostly your fault?

_____

_____

_____

**9.** Once people acknowledge they are stubborn, why would they put stubbornness ahead of family, friends, and career? _____

_____

_____

_____

## Chapter Two

# WHAT DOES STUBBORNNESS LOOK LIKE?

Art had no idea that he was much like the big, arm-waving, billowing, hot air balloon man down on the corner at the used car lot. The balloon man looked happy, fully alive, and bigger than any real person. He seemed full of control over the people who noticed him and were drawn to the lot to purchase a car. Everyone passing by saw him as he bounced around, full of life and vitality. When evening came, though, and the store closed down for the night, the owner unplugged the balloon man from his air source. He immediately fell flat on his face, unable to rise in his own power or even move one iota. What a perfect picture of Art! He was so blind to the truth of this song, "Without Him [Jesus] I can do nothing; without Him I'm sure to fail."

Art used his stubbornness to make himself feel strong, powerful, and in control. After all, his ways looked so good, so wise, and so perfect. "Why wouldn't everyone want to follow them?" he thought to himself. There was something comforting and satisfying in being right. It felt safe to follow his own thought processes and not have to depend on or trust in anyone else. He overlooked the verse in Proverbs 14:12 that says, *"There is a path before each person that seems right, but it ends in death."*

A 12-year-old boy in Art's family said to him one time, "Stubbornness is the **stupid** part of determination." Art refused to listen to that wisdom or ponder its impact on the way he was living his life. "How could I be acting stupidly when my thoughts and plans are so right and good? I know I'm not being stupid," He assured himself. Art didn't realize that God saw his heart and had this to say about his thought processes in Romans 1:22, *"Claiming to be wise, they instead became utter fools."*

Art didn't understand that stubbornness is like an addiction – an addiction to his own thought processes. He was sure that having **his** way would give him everything he longed for, hoped for, and needed to make him happy, successful, and content. He believed with all his heart in the song that says, "If the dreams that I dream would come true, and the schemes that I scheme I could do, then it seems there would be contentment for me…" He used food to make himself feel better and as a stress reliever, and he was able to justify his behavior because it did seem to work. Food gave him something to look forward to, something to distract him from the fact that life wasn't turning out the way he had planned. Alcohol was tempting for the same reason. "Just a little," he rationalized. "Just enough to give me a break from my unfair life." Shopping also gave him a buzz of excitement. "A new grill could do wonders for my outlook on life," he reasoned. Creating something new, building something impressive, coming up with another great plan, focusing excessively on hobbies, using diversions to fill his time all fueled his need to feel

he refused to accept those decisions, or to be grateful for the help. Instead he would subtly resist and refuse to get on board with the plans. He would ignore or disdain the person who helped him. He would withdraw, go silent, hunker down, and shut others out of his world as punishment for daring to go against his will. Arthur was the kind of person that prompted some writer to pen these words, "Convince a fool against his will and he holds the same opinion still."

Art was in love with what he called "common sense." He was so proud of his ability to be practical and efficient, and he made sure everyone knew that his ideas were filled with common sense. What Art misunderstood was that God rarely uses common sense in the directives He commands us to follow. Art didn't comprehend that common sense is a human term, and that God's ways supersede common sense. It's almost impossible to find a situation in the Bible where the commands of God being followed had anything to do with common sense. "Build a boat in the middle of the field and fill it with two kinds of animals of every kind in the whole world? God, you have to be kidding!" "Pack up my belongings and family, and go to a place you'll tell me when I get there?" "You want me to go visit a king who wants to kill me? You want me to convince him to free two million slaves when I'm not even good at speaking?" "You want us to **walk** across a huge river?" "I'm supposed to fight an enormous army with 300 men?" "You want me to pray facing my open window in front of everyone when the punishment involves being thrown into the lions' den? Hello, is there anyone else up there??"

Because Art clung to common sense so tightly, God was rarely able to use him for kingdom purposes. He didn't understand that the only way to find true contentment and direction from the Lord was to follow Proverbs 3:5-6 with his whole heart – not common sense! (*"Trust in the Lord with all your heart; do not depend on your own understanding. Seek His will in all you do, and He will show you which path to take."*) As a result, Art missed out on many of the facets of the wonderful plan God had for his life.

-------------------------------------------

**1.** Do you find yourself defaulting to self–sufficiency? Do you hold common sense in high regard? Why or why not?

_____

_____

_____

**2.** Are there any areas in your life where you stubbornly cling to some sort of harmful behavior in an endeavor to feel better about yourself or life in general? If so, what are they? _____

_____

_____

_____

**3.** How often do you feel that if people would just do things your way, or if God would just go along with your plans that life would turn out so much better? Explain.

_____

_____

_____

_____

**4.** On a scale of 0 – 10 how well do you listen and communicate appropriate information to your friends, family, coworkers? Explain. _____

_____

_____

_____

**5.** How do you handle it if people don't listen to you and you're forced into a "majority rules" situation? Explain.

_____

_____

_____

**6.** What percentage of your time is spent caring for the needs of others at the expense of your own agenda? How effectively are you able to hear God's voice guiding you on how and when to reach out to those around you in difficult circumstances? _____

_____

_____

_____

**7.** How do you feel about Noah, Abraham, Gideon, Daniel? Do you admire their abilities to set aside common sense and strike out in faith? Explain. _____

_____

_____

_____

**8.** Do you have disdain, fear, or apprehension for living a life of uncertainty (through faith) apart from common sense? Why or why not? _____

_____

_____

_____


**9.** How often do you cling to self-sufficiency and common sense to chart your pathway? Why? How are those choices working for you? _____

_____

_____

_____


**10.** What do you think about faith? What does the Bible say about how to get more of it? Would you be willing to seek to live by faith rather than by common sense and/or self-sufficiency? Why or why not? _____

_____

_____

_____

## Chapter Three

# STUBBORNNESS AND LAZINESS ARE PARTNERS

Not only did Arthur refuse to accept the label of stubbornness, he definitely disagreed with the idea that he could possibly be lazy. He worked hard at his job, kept his yard nice and neat, did all the repairs around the house, and served on numerous committees at church. As he did with stubbornness, he refused to understand the deeper meaning of laziness (**doing only what I want to do WHEN I want to do it**). Art developed a lazy mind from not having to do consistent, age-appropriate, adult-supervised chores from the time he was a young child, and from not having to do anything he didn't feel like doing (i.e. Not being made to always be polite and respectful, not having to consistently use good manners, not being forced to talk and to answer appropriately when spoken to, etc.). A lazy mind can show up in many ways: a messy house or garage (things are not picked up or put away because there's no desire to do so at the moment – I don't FEEL like it); not taking care of possessions; watching TV instead of doing the things God desires (i.e. communicating with spouse, playing with or reading to kids, reaching out to needy friends, doing "kingdom" work); focusing on certain activities that are more fun, or will bring praise and recognition, while minimizing other activities that are actually more important in the long run (i.e. spending suitable amounts of time with spouse and kids, and doing the things necessary to appropriately care for spouse and kids – cooking, cleaning, laundry, fixing things when asked); not exercising appropriately; not controlling food intake; not consistently following rules or laws when they don't seem important, or justifiable, etc.

A lazy mind was certainly present at the core of Art's being when he didn't want to think about any issues, let alone deal with them, if they seemed too painful, scary, or too hard to change. He always took the easy way out and just ignored the problems instead of searching for solutions. The lazy approach allowed him to pretend that everything in his life was fine. He could feel happy and satisfied, and have a sense that all was well. Art didn't understand that by ignoring problems, glossing over them, or dismissing them as "not so bad", he was actually **lying** to himself. Hand in hand with stubbornness, his lazy mind allowed him to overlook the verse in Proverbs 28:14 that says, *"Blessed are those who fear to do wrong, but the stubborn are headed for serious trouble."*

A lazy mind caused Art to pass his problems onto other people hoping they would step up and deal with them. He wanted the school and his church to teach and train his kids so **he** wouldn't have to put forth the effort. He wanted his boss to fix all the issues at work so **he** wouldn't have to pray, spend time in research, and pick other people's brains to find solutions. He wanted the government to come up with all the answers to society's ills so **he** wouldn't have to become involved.

A lazy mind prompted Art to never set New Year's resolutions. He said it was because setting resolutions was a stupid idea, but the real reason was that he didn't want to expend the time or energy to actually change. He didn't want to learn new information, stretch and grow in his occupation, develop his talents and abilities according to God's will, or become a healthier person.

A lazy mind helped Art defend the philosophy he modeled to his kids: "Do as I say, not as I do." It would be way too hard to actually show by his example what he was attempting to teach them. "Besides," he justified, "They need to learn these good habits while they're still children. It doesn't matter if I don't follow my own advice because I already have all of life figured out and know what I'm doing." By refusing to follow his own belief system, he was allowing laziness to make him "slip up" in his supposedly firmly held convictions ; something everyone else but Art was able to see.

A lazy mind enabled Art to absolve himself of any guilt for working mostly on his own ideas and plans instead of concentrating on activities his wife might enjoy doing with him. He said to himself, "I'm doing this project for her. She should be grateful that I'm such a creative, diligent husband." He didn't care that his wife's needs and desires were not being met even though he promised on his wedding day that he would put her first.

A lazy mind kept Art from observing his kids in a way that would allow him to learn their likes and dislikes. It prevented him from seeking them out and doing the kinds of things with them that they enjoyed doing. "They would probably rather spend time with their friends than me, anyway," he rationalized. "I'd just be in the way." He didn't see the heartache coming down the road when they began to exclude him from their lives just as he had been excluding them from his life.

A lazy mind helped Art justify his lack of time and attention to the needs of his employees. "After all," he maintained to himself, "I pay them a good salary. I can't be bothered with their complaints." It didn't dawn on him that when his employees began to treat him with disdain and a lack of loyalty, they did so because of his own choice to neglect them.

A lazy mind allowed Art to excuse his decision not to actively seek God's direction for His life. "He should just be glad I'm doing all these activities for Him. It would take too much time and effort to actually figure out God's will, so I'm sure He's okay with me just doing what I think He wants me to do. Besides, I know God wants me to be happy, and I'm doing what makes me happy," he reminded himself every time He was tempted to seek the Lord with all his heart.

Because Art refused to see problems coming on the horizon and took the easy way out in every situation, he was woefully unprepared when the storms of life began to pummel him.

--------------------------------------------

**1.** Do you think you struggle with a lazy mind based on this deeper definition? Why or why not? _____

_____

_____

_____

**2.** What problems have you faced that you've taken the easy way out in handling? What was the result? _____

_____

_____

_____

**3.** Have you ever ignored an issue hoping it would go away or someone else would fix it? If so, what was the result?

_____

_____

_____

**4.** What do you see as the consequences if you don't deal appropriately and quickly with this fault in your life?

_____

_____

_____

**5.** Why is a lazy mind such a hard condition to overcome? Does laziness perpetuate laziness? Why or why not?

_____

_____

_____

**6.** What steps would have to be taken in order to change a lazy mind into a diligent, self-disciplined mind? Could it be done without an accountability partner? Why? _____

_____

_____

_____

**7.** What would have to take place in your life in order to bring you to the point of being willing to change in any area of your life that needs a new direction? _____

_____

_____

_____

**8.** Have you faced any storms of life yet? If so, how well prepared were you to deal with them? Explain.

_____

_____

_____

## Chapter Four

# CREATE THE PERFECT STORM: ADD SELFISHNESS

Art would never call himself selfish because he did things for other people all the time. He helped his elderly neighbors, he gave to charities, and he worked on the serving teams at church. He didn't understand that his "serving" was done with a motive to look good, to convince himself that he was following God's rules, and to fill a desire in him to be needed and valued. His focus was on his own thoughts, doing things his way, and meeting the goals he had set, and he didn't realize that his "self" focus was the same as selfishness.

Art was always looking out for what was best for him, or what **he** thought was best for others. He didn't comprehend that when he honored his own thought processes above others or in place of God's will for his life that he automatically became a selfish person. He was unable to see the ridiculousness of thinking that he, as a finite person, could ever know the future, have any real wisdom, or have the strength to make good choices on his own. He overlooked the scripture that says we're to ask

**God** for wisdom. That directive implies that while we need wisdom, we don't have any and can't get it on our own.

Because Art thought first and foremost in every situation of how **he** would be affected, he soon forgot what God's plan was for His children. II Corinthians 5:15 says, *"He died for everyone so that those who receive His new life will no longer live for themselves. Instead, they will live for Christ, who died and was raised for them."* Art's selfish focus caused him to value himself above others. "I deserve to be treated as important," he said. "I deserve these things I want to buy. I deserve a nicer house. I deserve more money and a better wife, kids and boss. I deserve this promotion and the corner office." As his selfishness grew, so did his anger and dissatisfaction with his lot in life. He developed an entitlement attitude and made sure everyone around him knew how much he was worth.

Art's selfishness caused him to show a spirit of irritation and impatience to those around him including his children. Because he wanted to be in control and have everything go his way, he got very frustrated if his kids interrupted his train of thought, if they made a mess that he had to clean up, or if they got in trouble at school. He scolded his wife if the house wasn't clean enough, if the meals weren't up to his standard, or if she hadn't completed all tasks he thought she should have done to make his life easier. He was irritated with his employees if a deadline was missed, if orders weren't filled fast enough, if the company didn't grow as fast as he thought it should, or if they forgot his birthday. He was impatient while driving, continually exceeding the speed limit, and then yelling and honking his horn at everyone else who didn't get out of his way. He was impatient with God who didn't answer his prayers fast enough or in the right ways. In fact, irritation and impatience became a way of life for Art.

Art's selfishness became more and more apparent as he plowed ahead over anyone's objections and did whatever he wanted to do in life. He was determined to make his plans work so he indulged in the futility of "doing the same things over and over hoping for different outcomes", or of trying different plans and ideas hoping they would bring him happiness. He didn't seek out his kids and hang out with them even though he knew he was supposed to as a good father. He didn't ask what they wanted to do, look for ways to encourage or pleasantly surprise them, or fit himself into their worlds. He certainly didn't humble himself enough to seek his wife's counsel or advice, or to plan activities she would like; that would take too much effort and perhaps even cause him to feel uncomfortable. He ignored the verse that says in Ephesians 5:21, *"And further, submit to one another out of reverence for Christ."* He didn't listen to his employees' ideas or suggestions. After all, he was the boss and knew best. He saw his life as a stage where he was the main character in the drama he had planned, and everyone else's role in this production was to meet his needs.

One day, much to his shock and sorrow, Art realized that he was the only one left on his "stage."

-------------------------------------------

1. Is it possible you could be selfish? Explain. _____
_____
_____
_____

**2.** How would your friends/family rate you? Why? _____

_____

_____

_____

**3.** What causes people to choose to be selfish when God commands us to have a servant's heart? _____

_____

_____

_____

**4.** Why is selfishness so easy to justify? _____

_____

_____

_____

**5.** What's the difference between being selfish, and having a good self-esteem? _____

_____

_____

_____

**6.** What do you think is the antidote for selfishness? Why would that work? _____

_____

_____

_____

**7.** Have you ever acted out of selfishness? If so, what was the result? Were you happy with it? _____

_____

_____

_____

**8.** On a scale of 0 – 10, how often do you find yourself speaking in an irritated, impatient tone of voice? Why? What impact does that tone of voice have on your family, friends, and co-workers? _____

_____

_____

_____

**9.** What do your driving habits show about your level of selfishness? Explain. _____

_____

_____

_____

# Chapter Five

## DOWNFALLS OF STUBBORNNESS

Because Art trusted in his own thought process above anything or anyone else, he used it to justify his wrong behavior. He used food to soothe his emotions and bring him a sense of enjoyment in life. He used alcohol to dull the pain and make him feel relaxed and happy. He watched too much TV in an effort to drown out his disintegrating life. He watched programs that gave him a thrill to make him feel like he was living life with "gusto". He spent money trying to gain an adrenaline rush of power and importance. The day finally came when Art noticed that his health was deteriorating and that his bank account was in dire straits.

In order to authenticate his own thought process and his obedience to it, Art couldn't listen to anyone else's counsel or advice. He missed out on all the great wisdom available for his journey through life. He could have learned from others' mistakes; instead he had to stumble and fall and bear the consequences of not listening to the experienced people God put in his pathway to help him avoid the pitfalls along the way.

Art had to avoid the tremendous wealth of guidance and direction in God's word, because if it didn't agree with his own perception, he had to ignore it. He could have had such a different life if he'd embraced God's principles instead of his own. He lost out on the "abundant life" because of his stubbornness.

Art didn't realize the problem with embracing stubbornness was that the consequences are often not seen until down the road when disaster strikes. Every little act done on his own and every word spoken without the consent of the Holy Spirit seemed fine. He thought he was doing well on his own and that he could get away with ignoring God's directives. The problem was that every step Art took on his own was a step away from God. He didn't understand that his disobedience resulted in him not learning a lesson he would need in the future to by-pass a pitfall, not gaining wisdom he would need to navigate an up-coming crisis, not building the character he was going to need for the next battle, not engaging in the activity of putting on the whole armor of God so he would be ready to stand firm. Consequently, Art was completely unprepared for the spiritual onslaught from his enemy – the devil. He slipped, he fell, and at times he completely caved in - totally at the mercy of the Evil One.

Art had to view everything through the lens of right or wrong, black or white. He had to be completely right in order to support his view of himself as worthy to be his own god, so there was no room for other people's ideas or opinions. He only read books or listened to speakers who believed the same way he did. He was desperate to find support for his own thought processes so he could prove he was right and everyone who differed with him was on the wrong track! At times he was forced to go along with other people's viewpoints, but he watched carefully and bided his time until he could prove their way to be false. He hoped for their failure! He never understood the great gift God had given him in friendships. God says in Proverbs 27:17, "As iron sharpens iron, so a friend sharpens a friend." Art forfeited this wonderful tool for growth in his life. He followed the philosophy of "I'm okay – you're not okay," in the OK-Not OK Matrix developed by Frank Ernst. Ernst said this about people like Art: "People in this position feel themselves superior in some way to others, who are seen as inferior and not OK. As a result, they may be contemptuous and quick to anger. Their talk about others will be smug and supercilious, contrasting their own relative perfection with the limitation of others." Obviously, Art's belief system was not popular with his family, friends, or co-workers.

Art was never able to love his wife as God commanded him to, because he viewed her as his assistant, only useful to meet his needs and help him become successful. Instead, she became the source of his biggest frustration and disappointment because she eventually rejected his treatment of her. This outcome would result in the life of a stubborn woman, too, because she could never submit to her husband after setting herself up as her "god". Submission would not be in her vocabulary or part of her plans for her life.

Art believed, for the sake of justifying his self-addiction, that God helps those who help themselves. He worked hard at his "trial and error" philosophy so he could figure everything out on his own and take the credit. He missed out on all the wisdom God would have given him because he refused to humble himself enough to ask. (*"If any of you lacks wisdom, he should ask God, who gives generously to all without finding fault, and it will be given to him."* James 1:5).

Art didn't realize that when he chose to make his thoughts the "right" thoughts, he was being disrespectful to the God who made all people with their various strengths and personalities. When he looked down on everyone who didn't think or act the way he thought they should, and when he tried to control others, he was insulting the God who made each person unique, and who formed them in His own image. Art should have been scared to death of the consequences of attempting to speak for God into other people's lives without asking Him for wisdom. Instead he forged ahead with his "god complex" alienating people as he went.

Art's choice to be stubborn set him on a collision course with the refiner's fire built to burn off all the dross in his life. A refiner's fire has to be intensely hot in order to burn away all the impurities; the heat is brutal on the dross – no impurities survive that process because the heat is applied for as long as is necessary to purify the gold (or in this case, Art's faith in God). Because God's love for Art was so great, He was willing to go to any lengths to turn Art's heart away from self-love to full and complete love for His Heavenly Father. Romans 2:5-6 says, *"But because you are stubborn and refuse to turn from your sin, you are storing up terrible punishment for yourself."*

The only way Art could view himself as "god" was to have a following of people who would support his ideas and thoughts, and then attempt to obey him. He set up his own kingdom starting with his wife and kids, and extending it to whomever he could find to control. The people he sought to control were those who were insecure, fearful, and willing to latch onto someone who would tell them what to do. Amazingly enough, Art was able to spot these people a mile away, and to present himself as their rescuer. He came across as confident, knowledgeable, and dependable. The frustrating part for those attempting to follow him, though, was his lack of consistency. He would add things to their list of rules to follow, and he was never satisfied with their level of adherence to his guidelines. Often, he would take them to task for not obeying him for something he'd never communicated to them in the first place. He was always angry and frustrated with his "subjects" because they could never please him enough or follow his ideas as closely as he pictured they would. When his family and friends finally left him, he lost everything including his kingdom and his throne. (Proverbs 29:1, "*One who is often reproved, yet remains stubborn, will suddenly be broken beyond healing.*")

Art said he didn't care. Now he was free of all those hindrances that got in his way and slowed him down from meeting his goals. He was surprised at how lonely he was, though, and how dissatisfied he became at just living for himself.

------------------------------------------

1. Are any of these downfalls of stubbornness true in your life? If so, which ones? _____

_____

_____

_____

2. On a scale of 0 – 10 how hard is it for you to listen and learn from other people? Why? _____

_____

_____

_____

**3.** Is there anything in your life that you use to make yourself feel happier? Anything that now has mastery over you? If so, what is it? _____

_____

_____

_____

**4.** How often do you challenge yourself to learn something new or to actually consider an opinion that's different from your own tightly held viewpoint? What does that feel like? _____

_____

_____

_____

**5.** How many of your friends, family, and acquaintances believe differently than you do on various topics? How do you handle those differences? _____

_____

_____

_____

**6.** Have you ever felt gleeful when someone who disagreed with you was proved wrong, and you were right? How important is it to you to always be right? Explain.

_____

_____

_____

**7.** What negative consequences of stubbornness have you seen in your life or in the lives of those around you? Have you ever felt "the refiner's fire" in your life? Explain.

_____

_____

_____

**8.** Do you ever find yourself looking down on other people, or using your own thought processes as a "standard" that everyone should follow? Why or why not? _____

_____

_____

_____

## Chapter Six

# Playing the Blame Game

Art used his superior intelligence to perfect his habit of placing blame for anything that went wrong with his plans onto those around him. He maneuvered, dodged, hemmed and hawed, and, yes, even lied his way out of having to face the truth about himself. Of course, he could justify his actions and words as being close enough to the truth to be acceptable even if his "little white lies" hurt those around him. He spent very little time looking inwardly as the scriptures command (Psalms 139:23-24, *"Search me, O God, and know my heart; test me and know my anxious thoughts. Point out anything in me that offends you, and lead me along the path of everlasting life."* ), and the rest of his time focused on blaming others or circumstances for the issues in his life.

Art told his wife that if she would just submit to him like the Bible commands, everything would be fine. He'd shake his head at her foolishness if she dared suggest a different plan than the one he purposed. He wondered why God hadn't blessed him with a more supportive helpmeet that could assist him in reaching his full potential.

He painstakingly spelled out her faults in the hopes that she would see the error of her ways and follow his God-given right to be the leader in his home. The idea of a partnership where each person had talents and abilities to bring to the table, and that each idea was worth listening to, praying about, and discussing was foreign to his way of thinking. That scenario would have completely ruined the great opportunities he had to be in charge of those around him.

If Art's kids messed up in anyway, he blamed it on society, the poor school system, his dysfunctional church, his wife's ineptitude as a parent, or the fact that he had been "blessed" with inferior kids. The thought that anything he might have done or said could have contributed to their wrong behavior never crossed his mind. Instead, he made sure they understood how their bad behavior had embarrassed and disappointed him, and how their inappropriate attitudes and actions made his life more difficult.

If his employees made mistakes, he pointed out their flaws in front of others in an effort to show them the error of their ways. He made sure he communicated his superior thoughts, and how he would have handled a particular situation if he were in their place. He let them know how much their mistakes had negatively affected him as their boss, and advised them that the next time it happened their job would be in jeopardy. He gave no thought to the possibility that he might not have trained them correctly, given them the right tools to succeed, or provided them with enough information to make the right decision.

His friends came in for their share of blame as he showed his irritation and impatience at their inferior behavior and plans. If they had a problem or fell into temptation, he had nothing but scorn for their weaknesses. It never dawned on him that giving his support and encouragement could have helped his friends be more successful. It also never crossed his mind that he might be making the same kinds of mistakes, and just be more successful in covering them up or in not getting caught.

Of course, God deserved blame, too, from Art's perspective. "Why is my wife so hard to control and so unsupportive," Art railed at God. "I asked if it was your will to marry her and you gave me peace! Why haven't you changed her into the person I need her to be?" He often angrily confronted God, "Why aren't my children better behaved? It's not my fault because I did everything right. Where ARE you? Why aren't you answering my prayers for a better job, more money, a nicer boss? Why do I have so many problems? Where's your great power and strength that I read about in the Bible? Why are you so distant and uncaring?"

Art refused to look at his own failures because, of course, they weren't his fault. There was always someone or something else he thought worthy to receive the blame. If he forgot to do something, it was whoever's fault he deemed to be responsible for reminding him. If he made a mistake, he blamed it on the fact that he was too busy and other people weren't helping him out enough or carrying their fair share of the load. If he exceeded the speed limit and got pulled over, it was the fault of the other person in the car talking to him causing him to be distracted. Because of his practice of passing the blame onto others, he became proficient in covering his own faults. He conveniently forgot the verse in Romans 2:1, "*You, therefore, have no excuse, you who pass judgment on someone else, for at whatever point*

*you judge the other, you are condemning yourself, because
you who pass judgment do the same things."*

-------------------------------------------

**1.** Have you ever caught yourself blaming someone or
something for a situation that was clearly your fault? If
so, what prompted that response? _____

_____

_____

_____

**2.** How do those around you react to being blamed for
your problems or failures? _____

_____

_____

_____

**3.** Have you ever found yourself telling a "little white
lie" to get yourself off the hook if you thought telling the
truth might get you in trouble? What was the result, and
how did you feel about your lie? _____

_____

_____

_____

**4.** How does it feel to take full responsibility for your
actions without accusing anyone else even if they were
legitimately at fault, too? _____

_____

_____

_____

**5.** How do others respond to you when you confess your part in a failure without dragging anyone else into the situation? _____

_____

_____

_____

**6.** How do you feel and react toward others who are fully honest about their faults instead of trying to cover them up? _____

_____

_____

_____

**7.** What kind of accountability would it take for you to always shoulder the blame for your words and behavior instead of foisting it off on others? _____

_____

_____

_____

**8.** In all honesty, have you ever blamed God for your problems? Have you ever felt like He was ignoring your pleas for help, or that He wasn't deserving of your trust because He didn't do things the way you thought He should? Explain. _____

_____

_____

_____

## Chapter Seven

# REFUSING ALL HELP

Art didn't understand that the reason his stubbornness was so hard to admit and deal with was because it was his **stubbornness** that was keeping him from dealing with his stubbornness. It allowed him to justify controlling others and events, and let him rationalize his need to play God. It kept him honoring his own thought processes above others or in place of God's will for his life.

Stubbornness prevented him from seeing the ridiculousness of thinking that he, as a finite person unable to know the future, had any real wisdom or understanding to make good choices on his own. It caused him to refuse to listen to others or humble himself before the Lord and seek to become wise by God's standards. It made him hard and inflexible like concrete, and it would take God's jackhammer of correction to ever set him free. No wonder the Bible speaks so harshly about stubbornness in I Samuel 15:23, *"Rebellion is as sinful as witchcraft, and stubbornness as bad as worshiping idols."*

John Ortberg, pastor and writer, describes it this way in his book, "The Life You've Always Wanted," "Stubbornness is the pride that causes us to shun correction. It renders us unable to stop defending ourselves. When someone points out an error or flaw, we evade or deny or blame someone else."

Art didn't know it but a good working definition of his stubbornness would be, **"I will be right and have things my way because I WANT to. I will refuse to hear the truth because it interferes with MY plans."** He felt his value and worth depended on him being right.

Many people tried to help Art throughout the years but he steadfastly refused their counsel. After all, once he set himself up as his "god", how could he possibly admit he needed help from others? He'd have to admit that his whole premise of self-sufficiency was wrong, and that his problems WERE his fault. He might have to change, and that was scary. He didn't see the ridiculousness of thinking he actually **was** self-sufficient - as if "self" could EVER be sufficient. He ignored the song that says it best, "Without Him I can do nothing. Without Him I'm sure to fail." He didn't understand that we're lost without the help of the Lord, and that we're so desperate for God. We have absolutely no hope unless He helps, sustains, and guides us. So, because Art didn't believe that he needed anyone including God, he continued to stubbornly resist any counsel or advice.

Sometimes he reacted to people's attempts to help him by becoming angry and pushing back. Other times he just distanced himself from anyone who tried to get too close and suggest that he needed help. Sometimes he would actually appear to really change, but the change was just the "window-dressing" variety. It looked good on the outside and made people watching him think he was improving, but it was all an act designed to give him some breathing room. Sometimes he would pretend to listen if the pressure got too great and he might end up looking bad if he refused help. He was even willing to go to counseling if it would get people off his case, but inside he continued to defend himself and cling to his self-addiction. He was like the child whose mother made him sit down when he wanted to stand. While he did sit down because of his fear of punishment, the child informed his mother that he was still standing up inside. Art felt like he would lose everything if he actually admitted he was wrong. Because he didn't trust anyone else including God, he became what the Bible calls a "Fool". Proverbs 12:15 describes Art perfectly, *"Fools think their own way is right, but the wise listen to others."* What a name for a person who prided himself on being so smart!

-------------------------------------------

1. On a scale of 0 – 10, rate what you believe is your level of defensiveness, and/or pretending when confronted with your faults. Explain. _____

_____

_____

_____

2. Have you ever felt that your value and worth depended on being right? How did you handle those feelings?

_____

_____

_____

**3.** Proverbs talks much about the description of a fool, and contrasts a fool with a wise person. Which person are you the most like? Explain. _____

_____

_____

_____

**4.** On a scale of 0 – 10, how easy would it be for you to go to a trusted friend or a counselor to seek help if you suspect or are sure you need it? What about if others say you need it? Explain. _____

_____

_____

_____

**5.** On a scale of 0 – 10, how easy would it be for you to share with others that you went for counseling? Why?

_____

_____

_____

**6.** How often do you indulge in "image management" (presenting yourself as better than you really are), competition and/or comparison activities in order to feel better about yourself? Explain. _____

_____

_____

_____

**7.** What percentage of the "positive" changes in your spiritual life are actually window-dressing kinds of changes, and how many are true, life-changing transformations? Explain. _____

_____

_____

_____

**8.** What would have to happen in your life for you to be willing to become completely transparent and authentic to yourself, your friends and family, and to God?

_____

_____

_____

**9.** How do you feel about the verse in James 5:16 that says, *"Confess your sins to each other and pray for each other so that you may be healed?"* What about the verse in Galatians 6:2 that says *"Share each other's burdens, and in this way obey the law of Christ?"* Why would God want us to do that? Would it destroy you to do that?

_____

_____

_____

## Chapter Eight

# THE BLINDNESS OF STUBBORNNESS

Art wouldn't accept that his problems were a result of his blind spots. He gave lip service to the idea, but even though blind spots are a universal problem, Art refused to acknowledge his flaws. God has given us His word and the counsel of other people to help us see what we can't see on our own, just as we all require the aid of a mirror or a camera to see our own faces. Art scoffed at the idea that he needed help from others. He rationalized that he knew himself better than anyone else so other people's opinions on how to improve him were of no value from his perspective.

One of Art's blind spots was his refusal to ever apologize. Why would he do such a ridiculous thing when his mind was his god? He always had an excuse for his behavior, or he found someone to blame, or he just ignored the issue hoping it would go away. He felt that apologizing was belittling and embarrassing, and to do so would weaken his standing in the eyes of those around him. Little did he know that just the opposite was true. Had he ever humbled himself and admitted his faults, he would have been greatly honored and respected. Instead, he was ignored, shunned, and pitied.

Another of Art's blind spots was his ability to take in knowledge with his mind but never move that wisdom into his heart where it would have changed his behavior. What happened as a result of his ability to compartmentalize his thoughts separately from his actions, was that he could self-righteously spout off Biblical truths, while being guilty of the very thing he was preaching against. He just never let the two areas of his life touch each other; otherwise he might have been forced to change.

Art was also able to see very clearly, or so he thought, what was wrong in other people's lives. He would earnestly attempt to help others see the error of their ways, so sure he was speaking for the Lord, never seeing that he was guilty of the same sin. Oh, it might have looked a little different – maybe it showed up in some other form, but the person he was scolding and chastising saw Art's faults clearly. Art wondered why no one would listen to his "wise" words of counsel, or praise him for his great perception. Art became the person Jesus was talking about when he said in Matthew 7:3-5, *"And why worry about a speck in your friend's eye when you have a log in your own? How can you think of saying to your friend, 'Let me help you get rid of that speck in your eye,' when you can't see past the log in your own eye? Hypocrite! First get rid of the log in your own eye; then you will see well enough to deal with the speck in your friend's eye."* Because of his blindness, Art couldn't see that his children were modeling after HIM. Their wrong behavior was but a reflection of his **own** faults. Oh, they may have acted a little differently than he did, but their core sins were the same. Instead of praying for God to shine a spotlight into his life and show him his faults so he could change, Art shipped his children off to relatives or friends hoping they could "fix" his kids for him. As he watched his kids drive off to visit yet another rescuer, he'd just shake his head and wonder what's wrong with kids these days. He had no clue that he, himself, was the problem and that he was responsible for his kids' disrespect of him and for the messes in their lives.

Art was oblivious to the fact that all humans have a strongman residing in the deepest part of our beings (some sort of specific sin as referenced in Hebrews 12:1, "… let us strip off every weight that slows us down, especially the sin that so easily trips us up…"). This strongman guides and influences everything we say and do; sometimes we're aware of this influence, but mostly it happens subconsciously. Art's particular strongman was laziness, and stubbornness was the door-keeper to that area of his life. Stubbornness kept him from dealing with the strongman of laziness, and so his laziness became a greater and more powerful influence in his life. He didn't comprehend that God wanted to reduce the strongman to a weakling, and bring him to his knees. There's no other way for God to have control of a person's life ( *"For who is powerful enough to enter the house of a strong man like Satan and plunder his goods? Only someone even stronger--someone who could tie him up and then plunder his house."* Matthew 18:29). Art also didn't understand that God and he were a powerful unit, and together could easily defeat the strongman in him. He just had to ask God to give him strength to resist the temptation to give into laziness, and to not stubbornly demand his own way (*"For I can do everything through Christ, who gives me strength."* Philippians 4:13). Art tried in his own strength to be a better person but he was distressfully unaware of how powerful Satan is to hang onto the footholds he's gained in our lives. The strongman doesn't like being restricted in his desires, and will fight harder and with greater tenacity to have his own way. Art began to realize that if he ever got on the same side as God, he would actually be fighting against his own desires, and he couldn't bring himself to do such a scary, uncomfortable thing. "What if God doesn't come through for me?", he worried. "What if it hurts too much to change? What if I lose everything I care about?" He didn't believe God's word where it says, "*We use God's mighty weapons, not worldly weapons, to knock down the strongholds of human reasoning and to destroy false arguments.*" (2 Corinthians 10:4). He also didn't believe that God could and would help him survive that process, and that he'd be so much happier without the strongman running his life. *("Each time He (The Lord) said, 'My grace is all you need. My power works best in weakness.' So now I am glad to boast about my weaknesses, so that the power of Christ can work through me."* 2 Corinthians 12:9).

Even though God spent much time in the book of Proverbs teaching us how to be wise and to overcome these blind spots, Art avoided that book like the plague. He didn't want to read verses like Proverbs 19:20, "*Get all the advice and instruction you can, so you will be wise the rest of your life.*" "Well, I would," grumbled Art when confronted with this verse, "If I could find any wise people to get it from." He didn't like **this** verse any better; Proverbs 8:33, "*Listen to my instruction and be wise; do not ignore it.*" He refused to read verses like Proverbs 1:5, "*Let the wise listen to these proverbs and become even wiser. Let those with understanding receive guidance,*" or Proverbs 9:9, " *Instruct* *a wise man and he will be wiser still; teach a righteous man and he will add to his learning."* Instead, because Art clung to his self-addiction, he became the "Fool" described by God himself: *"Fools have no interest in understanding; they only want to air their own opinions."* (Proverbs 18:2), and Proverbs 1:7, *"Fear of the Lord is the foundation of true knowledge, but fools despise wisdom and discipline."*

For such a smart man, Art had fallen very low through his stubborn desire to be in control of his life, and to be right at all costs.

-------------------------------------------

**1.** Do you have any blind spots? If so, what are they? How do you know what they are? _____

_____

_____

_____

**2.** On a scale of 0 – 10, how easy is it for you to accept criticism? Why? _____

_____

_____

_____

**3.** How comfortable and obedient are you to apologize when you've messed up or hurt someone? Why? _____

_____

_____

_____

**4.** How often do you invite honesty from others, asking them to shine a light on your blind spots? Why? _____

_____

_____

_____

**5.** How often do you attempt to share your wisdom and insights with others regarding their faults without being expressly invited to do so? Why? How well are your attempts received? _____

_____

_____

_____

**6.** What is the name of the strongman that controls your inner being? What sin is the door-keeper that allows the strongman to thrive in your life? Would your friends and family agree? Why or why not? _____

_____

_____

_____

**7.** On a scale of 0 – 10, how healthy is your strongman? What are you doing to decrease his size and influence?

_____

_____

_____

**8.** Would you be willing to do a study of Proverbs, contrasting the wise man with the foolish man so you could see which category you fit into? Why or why not?

_____

_____

_____

**9.** Have you ever observed your children acting out in a way that made you see yourself in them? How did that make you feel? _____

_____

_____

_____

**10.** How do you handle the fact that your children learn most of what they think, feel, and do from what you portray of your thoughts and feelings in front of them? How do you cope with the truth that your kids hear very little of what you say, but they are continuously watching and modeling after what you do? _____

_____

_____

_____

## Chapter Nine

# THE SPIRITUAL CONSEQUENCES OF STUBBORNNESS

Because Art was running his own life by following **his** agenda, instead of the Lord's agenda, he didn't realize he was wide open to Satan's influence. He didn't understand that he had only two choices in life: God's way or Satan's way. He thought there was a third choice: HIS way. He believed he could run his own life and stay clear of both God and Satan. He didn't comprehend the great power of Satan over his life when he was out from under the control and protection of the Holy Spirit. He also was clueless of God's great love for him, and the wisdom God wanted to shower on him. He didn't understand that God would give him the power and the freedom to become all his heart was longing for, and that only God could fill him with the contentment he'd been seeking his whole life. He missed out on life's greatest blessings because he turned his back on God's plans to follow his own foolishness.

Because Art chose the path of self-addiction, he had to ignore big chunks of scripture to continue with his plan of following his own thoughts (His self-addiction turned to self-destruction). The idea of humbling himself, as God commands in I Peter 5:6, *"So humble yourselves under the mighty power of God, and at the right time He will lift you up in honor,"* was very scary to him. He assumed God was like his parents: distant, busy, permissive, and certainly not trustworthy or dependable. "Why would I ever do something so ridiculous?" he asked himself. Art certainly didn't understand or believe the truth about God described in Jeremiah 29:11, *"For I know the plans I have for you,"* says the LORD. *"They are plans for good and not for disaster, to give you a future and a hope."* He couldn't imagine how God's plans could be better than his own. Therefore, he also disregarded God's commands in Proverbs 3:5 , *"Trust in the LORD with all your heart; do not depend on your own understanding."* "Where would I be in life," he reminded himself, "if I didn't depend on my own understanding? God gave us brains to use, didn't He?" Romans 12:3 was another verse Art completely overlooked, *"…Don't think you are better than you really are . Be honest in your evaluation of yourselves, measuring yourselves by the faith God has given us."* "My happiness and success depend on not following that verse," he thought. Then there was the verse in Philippians 2:3, *"…Be humble, thinking of others as better than yourselves."* That verse REALLY bugged him. "It doesn't even make sense," he complained to himself. "It makes it sound like God is in favor of low self-esteem." By the time Art was done "cutting" up his Bible into sections he could handle, he had very little left. He would only listen to pastors who talked about subjects he agreed with. He just bought books to read on topics he could support. He talked to people who would agree with his ideas, and no one else. He became a very narrow-minded person always having to wear blinders in order to assure himself that he was on the right path.

Art had no idea what his life looked like from God's perspective. God, through his word, had tried to show Art, but he wouldn't listen. Jesus tells a parable about the soil in a person's heart. He says there are four different kinds of soil: the first one is the hard pathway where, not only is a seed unable to nestle in and send down roots to begin growing, it gets picked off and eaten by the birds. The second kind of soil is the rocky soil where there's a little bit of dirt so the seed can start growing but there's not enough soil for the roots to expand and deepen as required for true growth. The roots hit the rocks under the shallow soil and eventually die. The third kind of soil is the one where there's plenty of soil, but it's been overtaken by weeds. The weeds steal all the moisture and nutrients so there's not enough to support the new growth, and it dies. None of these first three kinds of soil ever produce any actual fruit. The fourth kind of soil is the kind Jesus longs to see in our hearts, the kind that is rich and full of nutrients just waiting to embrace and nurture the seeds when they're planted. This type of soil produces a bountiful harvest of 30%, 60% or even 100%; the "much fruit" Jesus talks about in John 15:5, *"Yes, I am the vine; you are the branches. Those who remain in me, and I in them, will produce much fruit. For apart from me you can do nothing."*.

Art didn't understand that his stubbornness made the soil in his heart as hard as a well-trodden pathway. The seeds God sent his way through other people, circumstances, and God's word couldn't penetrate the hard soil, and they were quickly ignored by Art. He also didn't realize that his laziness made the soil in his heart into rocky soil. He'd hear something that sounded like a good idea and put it into practice. As soon as it became difficult to continue with the idea and make it a habit, though, Art quit trying. The seed quickly shriveled up and died from lack of attention. He had many good intentions, but lacked the self-discipline to follow through and let the seed flourish.

What Art didn't comprehend was that his self-addiction precluded him from producing any fruit in his life for God's kingdom. Even though he was busy about God's work and looked great from the outside, God was not being honored or obeyed. Just because Art did lots of wonderful things for the church and the community and the poor, the fact that he never asked what GOD wanted him to do with his time and money caused Art to become a spiritual failure. God stepped aside and allowed Art to run his own life, and he produced nothing of eternal value. He was the person described in the song, "Nothing but leaves for the Master. Oh how His loving heart grieves, when instead of the fruit He is seeking, we offer him nothing but leaves."

Art's life ended up in shambles because he didn't take this verse to heart; he had cut it out of his Bible, along with all the other ones he couldn't accept; *"We are all infected and impure with sin. When we display our righteous deeds, they are nothing but filthy rags. Like autumn leaves, we wither and fall, and our sins sweep us away like the wind."* Isaiah 64:6.

-------------------------------------------

**1.** How have you sought to protect yourself from Satan's attacks? How well are your methods working? _____

_____

_____

_____

**2.** How have you insulated yourself from the influence of God's word? _____

_____

_____

_____

**3.** Were you surprised to find out that there are only two choices, not three, of who will run your life? What percentage of the time do you think you've been attempting to run your own life? Were you aware that by default, Satan was running your life? _____

_____

_____

_____

**4.** What is your understanding of the need and the way to put on the whole armor of God? On a scale of 0 – 10, how well are you covered with God's armor? Explain.

_____

_____

_____

**5.** How well do you know, understand, believe, and act on the great love God has for you? Explain. _____

_____

_____

_____

**6.** Is there any scripture you're uncomfortable with or choose to ignore? If so, what is (are) it (they)? Why are you uncomfortable or choosing to ignore it (them)?

_____

_____

_____

**7.** How would you describe the soil in your heart? Why?

_____

_____

_____

**8.** On a scale of 0 – 10, what percentage of your actions and words are actually producing fruit for the Lord? How do you know if they are? _____

_____

_____

_____

**9.** How do you determine if the ministry and service you're involved in for the Lord is actually His will or just what you think you should be doing? Explain. _____

_____

_____

_____

**10.** What would it take for you to completely trust in the Lord instead of your own thought processes, and to do it all the time? Explain. _____

_____

_____

_____

## Chapter Ten

# THE FINAL OUTCOME

One day as Art was reviewing his life, listing his woes, and wondering for the umpteenth time what went wrong, he decided to actually take a look at himself and his so-called wonderful plans. He thought he could handle taking the risk to see if HE had made any mistakes. Art didn't know that God had been pursuing him all these years, and waiting for this exact moment as described in excerpts from the poem by Francis Thompson,

### THE HOUND OF HEAVEN

"I fled Him down the nights and down the days
I fled Him down the arches of the years
I fled Him down the labyrinthine ways
Of my own mind, and in the midst of tears
I hid from him, and under running laughter.
From those strong feet that followed, followed after
But with unhurrying chase and unperturbed pace,
Nigh and nigh draws the chase, with unperturbed pace.
Halts by me that Footfall.
Is my gloom, after all,

Shade of His hand, outstretched caressingly?
Ah, Fondest, Blindest, Weakest,
I am He whom thou seekest."

God finally saw the repentant attitude He was looking for, and had mercy on Art. Because of His great love, God had been doing a good work in Art through the discipline He sent his way. Art came face to face with a verse he had ignored all his life: *"For the Lord disciplines those He loves, and He punishes each one He accepts as His child."* God was thrilled with the progress He saw, and He began shining His powerful light onto Art's blind spots so he could see why his life was such a mess.

Art thought he was free and creative in running his own life, but God showed him that all his past experiences, all the way back to early childhood, had shaped him and molded his thought processes. His thoughts were not a product of his own ideas and great intellect after all. He was actually a captive to his corrupted mind! He saw that his mind was infected with a virus and was not in any way, shape, or form a reliable source to depend on or listen to for effective guidance. No wonder God says in Romans 12:2, *"Don't copy the behavior and customs of this world, but let God transform you into a new person by changing the way you think. Then you will learn to know God's will for you, which is good and pleasing and perfect."* Much to Art's shock and dismay, he realized that by choosing to be addicted to his own contaminated thought processes, he had become just like his parents whom he resented and distrusted. So much for running his own life and being in control!

At last Art began to realize that he was in deep trouble and helpless to fix his problems. Because his "soil " had not produced any crops, and because God loved him with a perfect love, Art saw that he must go through the process of having the soil in his heart plowed up and burned off as a farmer does when his field is not producing a good crop. He came to understand that stubbornness is only broken through pain. Just as gold has to go through the refiner's fire to burn off the dross, so he had to experience great pain to finally come to the end of his rope. Stubbornness has such addictive power that Art had to experience the same brokenness an addict does who is attempting to escape a drug addiction. He had to lose everything he held valuable and hit bottom before he would humble himself under the mighty hand of God. He recognized his need to start all over and learn how to do things God's way. Otherwise he would be like the person described in I Corinthians 3:15, "If it (his work) is burned up, he will suffer loss; he himself will be saved, but only as one escaping through the flames." (NIV)

Art found himself hating the fact that his life had turned out so badly, and longing intensely to be set free so he could become all God had planned for his life. He felt lonely, isolated and empty. He wondered if there was any chance for a "do-over." As he searched God's word that he was now hungry for and willing to obey, he found the answer, much to his great excitement: Ezekiel 36:26 says, *"And I will give you a new heart, and I will put a new spirit in you. I will take out your stony, stubborn heart and give you a tender, responsive heart."* Art cried for joy that there was hope for him, although he understood as with any kind of surgery, that the process would be painful and hard to endure. He didn't care! The glimpse of the ugliness in his soul and the understanding that it had indeed been HIS FAULT for the mess he was in, gave him the courage to sign up for God's surgery. He realized that God doesn't perform surgery on us without our full consent, and so, with a fearful heart but a strong determination, he handed over his will to His Heavenly Father. He whispered the words of the old song as he knelt before the Lord, "My stubborn will at last has yielded; I would be thine, and thine alone." He recognized that his words meant he was willing to climb up on the altar described in Romans 12:1, *"And so dear brothers and sisters, I plead with you to give your bodies to God because of all He has done for you. Let them be a living and holy sacrifice – the kind He will find acceptable."* To his great astonishment and joy, it was Jesus, Himself, the lover of his soul, who stepped forward to help him onto the altar and to perform the necessary surgery to make his heart tender and responsive.

Art finally met the "real" God who said this about Himself, *""The Spirit of the LORD is upon me, for he has anointed me to bring Good News to the poor. He has sent me to proclaim that captives will be released, that the blind will see, that the oppressed will be set free, and that the time of the Lord's favor has come."*

And so, "The Rock" was finally broken, the captive set free, and Art emerged from the wreckage of his life as soft, pliable clay in the hands of the Master Builder. His friends (yes, most of them accepted his humble, heartfelt apologies and renewed their relationships with him) renamed him "The Mighty Warrior." They said they had never seen anyone have as much power in battling against Satan's kingdom through prayer and humble obedience to the Holy Spirit as their friend, Art. He was still praying for reconciliation to occur with his wife and children since he now understood the limitless power of God to do the seemingly impossible rebuilding of his life. He trusted God to do what He promised in Joel 2:25, *"The LORD says, "I will give you back what you lost to the swarming locusts, the hopping locusts, the stripping locusts, and the cutting locusts. It was I who sent this great destroying army against you."* He also embraced and depended on the verse in Ephesians 3:20, *"Now all glory to God, who is able, through His mighty power at work within us, to accomplish infinitely more than we might ask or think."* How grateful Art was that he now knew he could believe in and rely on every verse of scripture to comfort, guide, and teach him how to find God's will for his life. What a relief to no longer have to pretend he was happy depending on his own flawed thought process.

Art never forgot the great love and mercy God showed him by giving him another chance to make his life count for eternity. He realized that if he had come face to face with the Lord while he was stubbornly following his own way, he would have had to deal with the consequences of the wasted life he'd lived. He would have seen the glorious plans God prepared for him, including blessings and rewards, but it would have been too late to embrace them. He would have had to live for eternity with the intense regret and sorrow of his foolish stubbornness.

Art's progress toward following God's will instead of his own was a slow, painful process with many ups and downs in his journey toward godliness. He did notice, though, that the old pathways of his thought processes were dying out. He was no longer tempted continually to look at other's faults instead of his own. New pathways were being developed in his mind. He found himself being filled with love and compassion towards others instead of blaming them for his problems. Rather than being negative, he began to practice praising the Lord for His goodness. A heart of gratitude started cropping up and crowding out his complaining spirit.

When the pain of his punishment seemed overwhelming, Art clung to the truth in Job 5:17 – 18, *"But consider the joy of those corrected by God! Do not despise the discipline of the Almighty when you sin. For though He wounds, He also bandages. He strikes, but His hands also heal."* Art finally realized that while the refiner's fire had been painful, it had only burned away that which was displeasing to the Lord, that which hindered him from becoming all God planned for him to be. His faith had never been hurt by the fire, only strengthened into pure gold, worthy for the Master's use.

I know all these things about Art because he is my brother, my friend, my role-model, my enemy, and yes, he is me.

-------------------------------------------------

**1.** Have you ever observed yourself becoming like someone in your family that you dislike? If so, what did you do?

_____

_____

_____

**2.** Have you ever experienced pain as a result of disobedience? If so, did the pain turn you to God or were you resentful? _____

_____

_____

**3.** What would it take for you to actually climb on the altar of sacrifice and submit your whole will into the hands of the Lord? _____

_____

_____

_____

**4.** Have you ever made a decision to humble yourself under the mighty hand of God? If so, how is that going?

_____

_____

_____

**5.** What do you think of God's plan which is to let us make our own decisions to follow Him? Do you wish He would make it easier on you or force you in some way?

_____

_____

_____

**6.** Have you observed anyone or do you know anyone who is a fully devoted follower of Jesus Christ? If so, were you envious enough to join them? Explain. _____

_____

_____

_____

**7.** Have you ever sensed the Holy Spirit "pursuing" you as is described in "The Hound of Heaven?" Are you still running or have you let Him catch you? What has been the result of your choice? _____

_____

_____

_____

**8.** Could anyone call you a mighty warrior because of your powerful prayers resulting from your close connection to the Lord? Explain. _____

_____

_____

_____

**9.** How would you feel if you knew today was the day you would stand before the Lord? Would you be joyful or full of regrets? Does the idea of seeing God face-to-face spur you to make the hard choice of letting Him turn His flashlight onto your heart? Explain. _____

_____

_____

_____

**10.** What was the most impacting sentence, verse, paragraph, or chapter in this book? Why? _____

_____

_____

_____